•UNBROKEN CIRCLES•

The Campground of Martha's Vineyard

• UNBROKEN CIRCLES •

The Campground of Martha's Vineyard

PHOTOGRAPHS BY BETSY CORSIGLIA

TEXT BY MARY–JEAN MINER

AN IMAGO MUNDI BOOK

DAVID R. GODINE · PUBLISHER · BOSTON

AN IMAGO MUNDI BOOK

FIRST PUBLISHED IN 2000 BY DAVID R. GODINE, PUBLISHER

POST OFFICE BOX 450, JAFFREY, NEW HAMPSHIRE 03452

WWW.GODINE.COM

LIBRARY OF CONGRESS

CATALOGING-IN-PUBLICATION DATA

Unbroken Circles : the campground of Martha's Vineyard /

Photographs by Betsy Corsiglia ; text by Mary-Jean Miner. — 1st ed.

p. cm.

ISBN 1-56792-121-3 (hardcover, alk. paper)

1. Architecture, Domestic—Massachusetts—Oak Bluffs—Pictorial Works.

2. Gothic revival (Architecture)—United States—Pictorial Works

3. Martha's Vineyard Camp Meeting Association—History

4. Oak Bluffs (Mass.)—Buildings, structures, etc.—Pictorial Works.

I. Miner, Mary-Jean, 1937– II. Title

NA7235.M420183 2000

728´2´0974494—dc21   00–035435

• CONTENTS •

INTRODUCTION
page xi

SPRING
page 1

SUMMER
page 19

FALL
page 79

WINTER
page 101

THE PHOTOGRAPHS
page 119

Lithograph of Cottage City ca. 1875.

On the island of Martha's Vineyard in the town of Oak Bluffs there is a community of mostly summer residents who live in small Victorian style cottages that were all built in the years between 1859 and 1864. The architectural style is known as Carpenter Gothic, and the cottages, often original, are well-preserved and well-maintained. Very few villages, even in New England, display such consistency of style within their streets as this community known as the Martha's Vineyard Camp-meeting Association. The Association was founded by Methodists, whose religious style tended to be more outwardly expressive than that of the established churches that grew out of the Puritan tradition. The Campground provided a logistically remote setting where people could congregate in large numbers for long religious services among their own kind.

Surrounding the central, circular Tabernacle are gingerbread cottages in many colors adorned with varied jigsaw decorations. At the center is Trinity Circle, the avenue originally named Broadway, which then connects, like a spiderweb, with streets and paths describing still larger circles (see illustration on endpapers). Most of the houses are small and simple; a few over time have been enlarged or combined.

Originally each circle housed families from a particular church, perhaps from Providence or Fall River, and back when the Camp-meetings began in 1835 and the housing was temporary, the circles started out as tent sites. Parishoners arrived from countless familiar locations in Massachusetts, Rhode Island, and Connecticut. Imagine coming to the island, after a long, dusty journey and a ride on the steamship — perhaps an old side-wheeler, the *Martha's Vineyard* or *Island Home*, which dropped passengers, coal, and lumber off at Highland Wharf, just a horsecart ride from the Campground — only to have to set up your own tent before dropping off to sleep on piles of straw!

Visitors usually stayed for several days, listening to almost continuous preaching, at

The ferry Martha's Vineyard *discharging passengers at the Cottage City dock.*

At dockside the trolley picked up passengers bound for the Camp-meeting.

An early view of Siloam Avenue as seen from the dike road.

Lithograph of an early Camp-meeting, ca. 1860.

first in a large tent set up with a lectern, later in the iron-trussed Tabernacle, built at about the same time as the cottages.

Tents were stored in the loft of what is now the Association office, and there were other small storage areas spread around the grounds. By 1858, there were 150 tent sites and some of the new tents even had wooden walls and floors that were left from year to year. When more permanent camps became desirable, an early kind of prefabricated house began to appear, shipped on barges from the mainland. Cottages came in various stages of completion. Whole walls were created from green lumber, in dovetail fashion. Two posts without studs were set eight feet apart, and, as the wood seasoned, the joints became permanently welded together. Although the walls were durable, the cottages were never really intended as permanent homes, but most have stood the test of time and remain much as they were built. The walls have become a single unit; when a hurricane struck in the early 1990s, a tree fell across a wire and the entire wall pulled away as a single piece from the rest of the structure.

The Camp-meeting was originally founded in an unsettled part of what was then Edgartown. The area became known as Cottage City, and later was incorporated as Oak Bluffs. As the town developed and became more commercial, the Camp-meeting fathers built a six-foot high fence around their acreage. Gates were locked every evening in an effort to maintain Camp-meeting rules, which forbade smoking, drinking intoxicating beverages, and such sinful pursuits as card playing.

Today, the association's connection to Oak Bluffs is primarily through the services provided by the town. Owners of the cottages pay property taxes only on their dwellings, since the land is owned by the Association. Only those (perhaps thirty people) who claim their cottages as a primary residence are on the voting list. Unlike most of the Camp-

*Cottage on Clinton Avenue near the one where
President Grant stayed in 1874.*

ground streets, which face inward towards the Tabernacle, there are two streets on the circle's perimeter that face outward: Lake Street looks out over Oak Bluffs harbor, once known as Lake Anthony; and Siloam Avenue faces Sunset Lake. But the style of the houses on the perimeter is still consistent with those in the inner Campground. When Roberta Lowe and her husband John bought one of the Siloam Avenue houses, the sale included old photographs of the street without the house, and more recent ones taken after it was built. Roberta's grandmother once lived in a house nearby, not unusual for these Camp-meeting owners. Roberta's family is one of the few that go back to the original summer colonists.

The primary architectural style is Carpenter Gothic; the houses look like tiny little churches. Windows feature pointed or round arches, and the main entrance is usually a double door of similar style, opening inward. The cottages are embellished with unique jigsaw decorations of almost endless variety. The front porch runs the width of the house, and often a little balcony off the main upstairs bedroom juts out over the porch roof, where another pair of double doors allow furniture to be lifted to the upper rooms, as the stairways are often twisting and narrow.

Originally, the outer walls were vertical boards that served as both siding and interior walls. Today, some have natural or painted shingle siding; others are modified but retain the board-and-batten look.

In all, there are more than 300 cottages, some secluded within the maze, but most a highly visible part of the Campground scene. All are people's homes, whether used just during the summer season or, in a few cases, as the primary residence. Some have been insulated and winterized, but the original walls are intact in the interior — insulation was added to the outside, then replica siding attached. The Sonnenberg cottage, as well as "Blenheim" and "Tall Timbers," are examples of winterization. Some even have full cellars.

By 1853, less than twenty years after the very first meeting, there were 53 clergy and five to six thousand people in attendance. Five years later, the campground hosted some eight to ten thousand people, with 300 horses, yet it still had only one well! In 1864 the Camp-meeting purchased 26 acres of land at the site, and the Martha's Vineyard Camp-meeting Association was organized formally four years later. At that time the campers were all Methodist. By the twentieth century the association had become interdenominational, with many and diverse viewpoints expressed. When the Association was incorporated in 1868, the meetings were held around a preacher's lectern, and whale oil lanterns on posts provided the light around the circle. The iron-trussed Tabernacle, completed in 1879, provides the gathering spot for services and other programs, and it is now listed with the National Register of Historic Places. The Camp-meeting Association today welcomes thousands of visitors and several generations of returning residents each season, with programs and traditions that bring people back year after year. And the Campground is still maintained as a religious retreat, with newcomers asked to provide written recommendations from their religious leader attesting that they will participate in Camp-meeting programs.

At left, President Grant (seated far right) and his entourage during his visit to the Campground.

The gardens have started to show life before most of their gardeners arrive for the season. Brave little crocus and nodding daffodils cheer the scene; some residents manage a visit or two before settling in for the summer season, but many, arriving just in time for the daylilies, never see their iris in bloom.

Early visitors to Oak Bluffs are treated to a quiet little enclave that has not yet sprung to life. Even the busy main street, Circuit Avenue, is still a bit sleepy in the warm spring sun. For these fortunate vacationers, there is the welcome celebratory feeling that dreary winter is finally giving way to blossoms and scents borne on gentle breezes. Of course, this being New England, those gentle wafts may take on an unkind chill by late afternoon, when even the bright sun cannot warm the wind off the water. Compared to the mainland, our real spring comes late, and often rushes headlong into summer. It's cold, it's dreary; then it begins to warm, and suddenly it's too hot for woolens.

Campground resident John Lowe says, "When you see our porch chairs out, you'll know it's spring and we're back." Thus begins a new season of porch-sitting. Once the gardens are underway and the planters filled, the time has come for relaxing and visiting. Within the Campground, visiting has evolved into a ritual. Tom and Nikki Surr have perfected the routine. "We do a goodly amount of sitting here, with our feet up, visiting with neighbors and passersby," says Nikki. "It's the way we keep up with what's happening." Meredith Thayer says of Mrs. Rose, one of the oldest residents, who lived on the corner of Tabernacle Avenue, "I spoke to her every day for 35 years, as she sat on her porch, beginning every spring." When one family whose house was to be sold left the Association, their neighbor Elwood Preising could be seen each morning pausing just in front of the empty cottage, sadly shaking his head. His daily routine was a visit with his friend Earl on his Clinton Avenue porch. Elwood's trips to the post office have never been the same. With most families, part of each day is taken up with visiting, both on the way to town and back. It contributes to the community feeling, it develops into a predictable routine, and further suggests the closeness of Camp-meeting ties.

It's no wonder that so many first-time visitors ask what it takes to come here to live. And it's not just retirees who ask: a young couple, married one spring in the church on the Campground, spent the better part of a year visiting, looking for ways to make it possible to live here year-round. They came for Illumination, for Christmas, and again on Palm Sunday. A year later their first child was baptised in the Campground church where they had been married. Each year brings them closer to their goal.

3

4

8

11

14

17

SUMMER

From the years when horse-drawn carriages stopped at the corner of Clinton Avenue and Broadway, to the era of trolley cars circling the Tabernacle, to today, when automobiles arrive with luggage and furnishings on top and behind, the arrival of "The Season" means that population increases daily and that the Camp-meeting will once again become a summer community.

Shops on Circuit Avenue, which have been open weekends only, are cautiously initiating summer hours — first opening afternoons, then all day. Local musicians, who have been off "in America" earning a living during the winter so that they can return for the club season on the island, are starting to arrive, even before the summer boats begin to dock.

Then comes the day when, walking back from town and entering the Campground, whether from the entrance next to the firehouse, the Arcade, or the iron arch over Tabernacle Avenue, one again feels the change from the bustling center. The mood alters as abruptly as the wind direction. It's not exactly a hush, because there is almost always the sound of children playing. It's more a restful serenity, a feeling of peace; with just a few steps, you manage to get away from it all, to leave the "entertain me" atmosphere of Circuit Avenue for the inward calm of the Campground.

Robert Cleasby, a summer resident for every August he can remember, told his wife, Marietta, when they arrived for their first full summer, that the island "just didn't smell right." When she greeted this with disbelief, he explained, "No, I mean it; it just smells different in July." And he's right. In May, he would notice still another smell: flowering seasonal shrubs, lilac and wisteria determining the fragrance; by June and July honeysuckle has taken over, and in August it is privet hedge and rosa rugosa — the wild roses of the roadside hedges — that are in bloom. By late fall wild clematis, which clings to

any vertical surface on its journey toward the waning sun, gives a heady, rich scent to the crisp autumn days. But for now, we are still breathing summer air.

Here, young children are rarely bored. One reason is that their summer friends, whether they live on the island or just spend summers here, are seldom the same kids they play with at school. They enjoy their annual reunion; kids who don't spend much energy keeping in touch during the winter go on faith that their summer friends will soon be back and they'll pick up where they left off. They will explore the same places they've loved over the years, and when visitors return, they too must see all and do all. The same families have been returning here for years; their kids now have children and the next generation repeats the rituals.

As kids grow into teenagers, there are other needs. Income is required and summer jobs are sought. Years ago, youngsters dove for coins that travelers threw from docking or departing ferry boats. Though not exactly a career, it often led to other gainful employment. Meredith Thayer recalls that "girls worked at the movie theater; the really responsible job was ticket seller. You worked up from ushering." Stephen Shabica remembers, "We worked at the Wesley House all summer, with two days off — one every other week — waiting on tables for breakfast, lunch, and dinner, for $240 a week. Other boys worked in the kitchen or on the grounds crew." The shops on Circuit Avenue like Murdick's or Mad Martha's always have jobs to offer, providing you get there early enough.

Each summer cottages are spruced up, flowers planted, bedding aired, and rocking chairs repainted. Each house has its own personality. Tom and Nikki Surr are usually on their porch, with their feet up. The location of their cottage, *Wee Hoos*, is such that passersby are frequent, and they can tick off some general misconceptions about the Campground often heard from tour guides or speculating visitors: "The Tabernacle was once a railroad station; look, you can still see the tracks there, just in front of the Associ-

ation building." Or, "All these cottages are rentals," news that Kathy McKechnie, in the Camp-meeting office, is quick to contradict as she sends them on their way.

Wee Hoos's kitchen was once a shed where tents were stored from 1860 to 1867. Although most of Trinity Park was constructed in 1863-64, *Wee Hoos* was built in 1867 and attached to a shed that was no longer required for storage. The house features a rare piecrust arch, a form of interior gingerbread decoration used in only about a half-dozen houses in the Campground.

The Surrs recall old photos of the Campground showing a banner suggesting the whole story: "We'll camp a while in the wilderness and then we're going home." It is a message for everyone, whether taken literally or in a Biblical context. Never mind. Each year they return with the same feeling. "We'll camp for a while…" And in that annual interval, relationships grow deeper. There is a special commitment here, a way of becoming part of the Campground experience. Even those just visiting or renting a cottage for a few days or weeks manage to experience this feeling. The sense of community is strong, deeply felt, and widely shared.

Other recollections of the past come from old-timers like Curtis Collison, who has lived in the Campground since he was a young man. He tells about the days when cars were first ferried to the Island, "They were required to drain all the gas from the cars, putting it into containers. Of course, the cars and the containers came over on the same boat. I'm not sure what the point was." He and his wife settled their grandchildren into the cottage next door, and that wonderful feeling of family, steeped in the Camp-meeting lore, has passed down among several generations. Eric told us that in the good old days "Inez and Louise Phillips changed clothes three times a day." Albion Hart recounts another Campground myth: "People say that the cottages were small because people were so much shorter then. I tell them we water the furniture and it just expands to our size." But his

Barney the Shoosher

neighbor, Mr. DeLisle, points out that the door knobs *are* low to the ground. Albion maintains a water bowl for visiting dogs. "Squirrels and cats drink out of the birdbath," he says. And a most pristine birdbath it is. He adds, "My nephew put mahogany on the edges of the front porch. He has to have that trim on everything, being a sea-going type." The Harts' porch rails are designed to be removed when they need painting. They are attached by brass screws — no nails.

Before the cottages were built, each circle had its own Society Tent, where families shared space, with a curtain separating men from women. Later, communal meals were prepared and served there. Then, as new wells were drilled, individual tent sites were set up, each housing only one family.

Great care was taken to avoid fires at the tent site. Each family was allowed only one lantern, usually hung from the top of the tent. Every night a watchman went from tent to tent, making certain that the lanterns were extinguished. Even after electric lights replaced the oil lamps, watchmen continued to make rounds. Old-timers remember one in particular, known as Barney the Shoosher, who made certain that the noise level was kept down. His granddaughter, Anne Young, remembers Barney, who, even at age 78, still managed to keep watch all night, from ten until two. "He was so proud of his uniform," she recalls; "And he took his job so seriously." Anne was brought up by her grandparents and was a member of the second class to graduate from Martha's Vineyard Regional High School. She continued her tales of Barney: "People would say, 'Oh, no, here he comes!' At times he thought he was working for the FBI." The Surrs remember his words, "It's getting to be quiet time, now. You have to be quiet." Anita Buddington recalls, "We would tell naughty stories, and Barney the Shoosher would come around to quell the laughter. We'd pull in closer around the table, and the corny jokes would continue!" Tabernacle events are still finished at an early hour, but the gatherings at cottages continue well into the night. And Sully, the current watchman, is seldom called upon to keep a lid on the noise, although quiet time is still enforced.

The Society Tent was revived in a way in 1991 during the aftermath of Hurricane Bob. Power was out for several days and the Methodist church's parish house, with its gas stove, became the cooking tent. A pot of coffee was kept warm and families came by to cook their supper.

39

48

50

GRAND ILLUMINATION

"Paint the bottom first; that's what people will see," says Nancy Blank, supervising a lantern-painting session just before Grand Illumination night. As the kids drift away from the grownups and work unsupervised on their own masterpieces, there is considerable discussion about colors and techniques. Begun in 1869, the Grand Illumination is the high point of the Camp-meeting season; after this, activities and the business of the Camp-ground slip quietly and slowly down toward season's end. But in earlier years, Illumination signaled the *beginning* of the Camp-meeting year; lanterns were displayed and lit each night for a week, two weeks before the Camp-meeting actually began. In 1870, there were 750 lanterns; four years later, when President Grant visited, there were 3,200! In those days, the entire town of Cottage City, as Oak Bluffs was then called, displayed lanterns. In 1877, there was a marching band, boats were illuminated, and fireworks were set off. Nowadays, the Grand Illumination is held for only one night, usually in August.

Lanterns of paper and silk, treasured and stored away, or carefully painted the day before, are hung from porches and up along the eaves. In the early days, they were also strung between cottages, suggesting the connectedness of the campers. Many still light the lanterns in the traditional way, with candles set into beach sand to keep the flames contained; others rely on electric lights that don't require close attention from porch-sitters. And, reminiscent of earlier times, many dress in period costume, serving tea or peanut-butter cookies and punch on the porch to visitors who are often invited inside. Illumination is best experienced rather than described, as the Campground takes on a glow and the hospitality reaches out to thousands of passersby.

60

Preparations go on all day. The ceremonies begin with a band concert in the Tabernacle with excitement mounting as the daylight fades. At dusk, all lights are extinguished and the first lantern is lit, carried to the far end of the Tabernacle and hung in the entry arch. At this point the Tabernacle's electric lanterns are switched on, and folks at each cottage begin to light theirs. Thus the light spreads out, from the Tabernacle to the farther streets, and finally all the houses are illuminated.

Spectators stroll along the streets and lanes, talking with people on the porches, snapping pictures of a house decorated entirely with lanterns shaped like hot-air balloons, another with a model train winding about the garden, one with a moving ferris wheel, one where tea is being served, and several where pretty little girls in frilly dresses wave and grin, a favorable contrast to earlier times when families wearing the customary heavy, warm woolens sat stiffly for formal portraits.

A few years ago the family in one cottage had suffered a recent death, so their neighbors, anticipating the sorry prospect of a sad, dark home, made certain that a pitcher full of flowers was placed on the porch by the time the band began to play. On another occasion, when the cottage owner died suddenly just before Illumination, two of the summer tenants called the family and volunteered to come over to hang lanterns. It was a warmth shared, a life honored.

● PROGRAMS ●

During the early days of the Camp-meeting, the main focus for families was preaching, and speakers would hold forth for hours, several times a day. Over time, other programs were inaugurated: band concerts, choral programs, and even recitations. May Davies, an Englishwoman, developed a wonderful costumed storytelling series, with an outstanding interpretation of a World War I doughboy writing home his adventures in the service. She gave it up just a few years back when she found herself straying from the script. "I just can't seem to remember things in the right order," she said. Still in her eighties, she walked every day to the post office, and on Sunday to the Methodist church. The distinguished pianist and soloist Catherine Carver Burton, a graduate of Juilliard, was accompanist to church services and music programs in the Tabernacle. Her successor, Raymond Young, presents annual duet concerts with his son Stefan, a pianist and composer. David Crohan, the blind pianist from Rhode Island, returns each summer around Independence Day for at least one concert, playing the classics and improvisational pops. He weaves a tapestry of all-American tunes, covering the period of history of the Camp-meeting itself, from the Civil War to today's tunes. Choral groups, Gilbert and Sullivan productions, and community sings, held weekly under the direction of Robert Cleasby, round out the musical offerings.

Roque Avenue was named after the croquet-like game that was allowed, albeit grudgingly, by the management and only if kept distant from the Campground center. Though no longer used, that playground is still distinguishable at the outer limits of the Campground off Duke's County Road. Croquet tournaments were recently reinstated on the lawns around the Tabernacle.

It was many years before card-playing and other pastimes regarded as frivolous or sinful were finally allowed by the Camp-meeting. In earlier times, if people broke the rules, the miscreants were invited to pack up their dwelling and leave. And many did. Cottages that were once part of the Campground were sometimes moved by oxcart to neighborhood fringes, where the occasional glass of wine was tolerated.

● WORSHIP SERVICES ●

Gone are the days when preachers droned on for hours. Now guest preachers from a wide range of denominations and avocations are invited for each of the summer Sundays. The Tabernacle choir consists of volunteers from the Campground and the town, and the personnel changes as visitors come and go. Distinguished guests are often part of the congregation. President Ulysses S. Grant stayed at the Bishop Haven cottage, on Clinton Avenue, when he visited the Campground in 1874. Photographs show him sitting out on the upper porch greeting passersby. His visit coincided with Illumination and he viewed the fireworks display from the Dr. Tucker House with its large, square tower on Ocean Park. Although he did attend worship services, he supposedly considered them too long and tedious, and once he found himself locked out of the grounds when he stepped out to smoke a cigar and drink his brandy. At that time the whole Camp-meeting was enclosed by an six-foot picket fence, and locked up promptly at ten. So the President of the United States was locked out, and no one knows exactly how he got back in.

President Clinton, on the other hand, went to Tabernacle services on each of his first two visits to Martha's Vineyard. His plans were not announced in advance, and when it was abruptly decided, the Secret Service said their job would be made easier if the Taber-

nacle area were enclosed; so neighbors on Trinity Circle and the association staff scrambled to hang large canvas curtains, formerly used to control access to paid events. The choir was rehearsed, and the President and his family were given a warm welcome. It was noted that, far from President Grant's discomfiture, Mr. Clinton never even opened his hymnal; he knew the verses to all the old familiar songs by heart. Many appreciated that the nation's chief executive seemed to fit right in with the rest of the congregation.

The August visits of the President changed the usual winding-down process as the end of Camp-meeting season approached. The visits provided one last flurry of excitement, then the First Family returned to Washington, and the Camp-meeting families began to turn off the water and electricity and head reluctantly to their winter homes. Jean Sternberg, mistress of "Tall Timbers," expressed it nostalgically, "I hate to see people leave. Early this morning I saw a car going down the road all loaded with bicycles. I don't even know those people, and I still feel sad."

• FALL •

The first to depart are teachers and families with children. The teachers leave early as they have to be back at their winter homes before Labor Day to get ready for classes. There's a quick exodus, and the streets are suddenly half-full. Something essential, a part of the basic fabric of life goes too, and those of us living here year-round turn to our own children to prepare them for school.

As asters, marigolds, and chrysanthemums anticipate the first frosts or the possibility of Indian summer, the slanting light and the early dusk bring back the reality of the changing season. Evenings are chilly even when the days stay deceptively warm and sunny. Rainy days may still be muggy, but evenings tell the truth. Windows are washed, rugs are shaken, porch furniture is stored away, and David's "Island House," where there's piano music all summer long, is shuttered and boarded up for the winter.

It's early October and it has been cool, but today it's all of seventy degrees, balmy, and the only clue to autumn is one young oak tree uncharacteristically ablaze in orange. Several of these young oaks, planted three years ago to replace the huge losses from Hurricane Bob, are among the first to change color. A scattering of acorns lies in the paths. Peter Dawley, in charge of Campground buildings and grounds, has been changing the globe lights around the Palladian window in the Tabernacle. The sky is too overcast for good photos and the air becomes perceptibly cooler. A jacket might help. But there's still enough sky-glow to shine through the brilliant colors of the stained glass windows — one row horizontal, the upper one vertical. As the breeze brings down more leaves, late-season visitors drift by, taking pictures of the remaining porch flowers. It's all passing sad — a wistful, gentle silence, interrupted only by another wind-shift, or the adjustment of an extension ladder, or a quiet observation: "See how the flowers are chosen to bring out the house's painted trim."

Outside, just beyond the arch to Circuit Avenue, large signs are being put out to greet

President Clinton, who is expected to visit the Island briefly; but no one knows if he is coming to Oak Bluffs. There are houses up for sale and we are expecting some young friends who might be interested. Meanwhile, the Shabicas are getting ready for their trip south for the winter. Always reluctant to leave, they are never among the first to go. Eleanor Shabica, whose parents, the Wrights, were the first of their generation to come to the Camp-meeting in 1918, now counts four generations since then. In 1920 the Wrights bought a cottage for $500. In 1941 Eleanor and her husband Tony could have purchased one nearby for only $200. When they finally bought, they borrowed from "our rich uncle Joe, a direct male descendant of Roger Williams," as Tony recalled. "He always wore a shirt, vest, and tie, a real gentleman. He died in 1966." Dressing up seems to have run in the family. Eleanor tells of times when "we'd all get dressed up and go uptown in our funny hats, never cracking a smile. We walked that way all over Circuit Avenue."

New families come and old families die out. All become part of the community, their homes reflecting the summer life. The kids collect shells that become permanent decorations on window sills or get arranged into collages. Art projects, entered in the Agricultural Fair, display fading ribbons of blue, red, and white. Every year Eleanor Shabica's recaned rocking chairs take prizes. One summer, her son Steve was laid up with a broken leg; he assembled a collage of corks, still proudly displayed with its winner's ribbon. "I've threatened everyone not to touch a thing until I die," Eleanor says, with a sly smile. It seems unlikely that they'd do anything even then. There are lifetimes of memories in every corner and on every shelf.

81

86

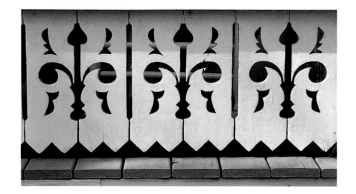

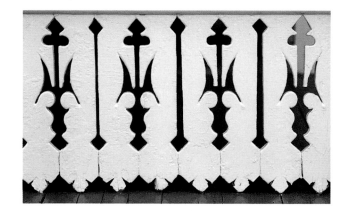

88

96

100

One by one, the little shops in town are closed. Only a handful will remain open all year. Eating out changes drastically. There's no waiting in line now, but the choice of restaurants is limited. The Campground itself is nearly silent. All the hundreds of Tabernacle chairs, bought years and years ago from Sears, Roebuck for a dollar apiece, are carefully stored away, and the Chickering grand piano goes into its yearly hibernation, not to reappear until spring.

There are many types of winters here on Martha's Vineyard. Most years, it is considered exciting if the snow falls long enough to keep the grass covered all night, before the rains come and all is brown and gray and dull again. Snow is a big event: island newcomers marvel at photographs of the harbor frozen over or driveways drifted in. There are chilly, brisk, snowy days, with the sky all lead and the water in the harbor showing through in dark contrast with the drifting white accumulation. Those days, the snow blows horizontally and children drag their sleds to the nearest hill to take advantage of the slidable, packable, buildable snow. On the Campground there is a hush, broken only by the scrape of a snow shovel, or the roar of Peter Dawley's snowplow, as the paths and doorways are cleared. Along toward evening, there may be a faint glow in the western sky, turning the rooftops pinkish, and suddenly everything starts to darken. Little indoor lights wink on in the occasional cottage. Amidst the stillness of the nearly deserted community, life continues, folks gather round the table for supper and perhaps later collect for a game of cards, or Scrabble, or Monopoly.

The Harts are at home. Along Rural Circle, Tara Bolash fills her bird feeders and calls the dogs back from their romp in the snow. Laura Gliga is just getting home from a rehearsal. And up on Clinton Avenue, Alice Turnell is getting ready to turn in. Lights wink off again and the stillness is deep and extended.

The next morning dawns brilliant and sunny and we all remember why we love being here in the winter. The quiet continues long into the morning, broken only by the bark of early-morning dogs and the screech of the wheeling gulls. Good mornings are exchanged as some hurry along to Linda Jean's to hear some storm stories and enjoy a big breakfast. The hearty smell of coffee greets them even before the door is opened. The day is consumed by clearing out driveways and doorways and trips to the post office and grocery store. By late afternoon, the sun sinks low and again all the world takes on a pink glow. The low angle of the sun creates contrasts not seen at any other time of year. The bright colors of summer cottages seem muted in the hush. Footsteps crunch again in the early morning.

The people who spend winter here become part of the larger community, frequent the post office, and visit over cups of tea. The summer people send Christmas cards from their winter homes. We send them pictures of their little cottages covered with snow. Over at the office, Kathy McKechnie readies schedules for the new season. Plans are made. The Campground waits. It won't be long before another spring. Then the circles of life will begin again and the shouts of children will be heard, along with the music — the continuing hum of a living, vital community.

106

114

THE PHOTOGRAPHS

2   *Albion and Cora Hart in the Victorian Garden.*

3   *The Tabernacle in early spring.*

4   *From her balcony Susan Fusaro greets Wendy Boothman, grounds gardener.*

5   *On his porch, Robert Harrell relaxes with pipe and paper.*

6   *The Ranslows' "Oops Cottage" viewed through the trees on Trinity Park.*

7   *Elwood Priesing resting.*

8   *Porch decor at the Phillips's cottage on Commonwealth Avenue.*

9   *Solveig and Randall Gerrard, Peter Dawley, Ralph Martell, and Earl Jacoby in consultation.*

10   *Svea Collison.*

11   *The welcome sign at the Calls' cottage on Trinity Park.*

12   *A welcoming doorway, and similar arched window with a view to Sunset Lake.*

13   *New and old styles combined in the dining area.*

14   *Wisteria envelops a balcony at Jordan Crossing.*

15   *Spring fence.*

16   *Irises in bloom at the Sonnenbergs' cottage. The resident canines, Nickey and Pokey, watch the passing scene.*

17   *An evening stroll past Trinity United Methodist Church.*

18   *Trees shade the lawn around the Tabernacle before a summer concert.*

20   *At "The Ark," Katie Firestone, reading, and Claire Pizzurro.*

22   *Tom and Nikki Surr chat with young Betsy Shabica, a regular visitor to the Wee Hoos.*

24   *Barney the Shoosher on patrol.*

26   *The Surrs' cat, Wilhemina, is named after their favorite queen, but they call her Bill.*

27   *Sarah Allen deep in the adventures of Harry Potter.*

28   *Elwood and Dorothy Priesing.*

29   *Eleanor and Tony Shabica.*

30   *Artist Marietta Cleasby at work in front of the Swindle cottage on Trinity Park.*

31   The Gerrards' home was originally built for two sisters. Here Randall Jr., Randall Sr., and Solveig share the porch with their yellow Lab, Kelly.

32   Walter Frey recanes a chair.

33   Beryl Frey, who designed the Memorial Garden, has to maintain it as well.

34, 35   The Collisons' porch, and Curtis Collison and his granddaughter, Abigail Svea Foss.

36   Tabetha McCartney and Pat O'Connor pay a visit on the porch.

37   An interior with oil lamp, looking out to Clinton Avenue.

38   Beryl Frey, grandson Xavier, and Watson.

39   An upstairs bedroom underneath the eaves.

40   David Hamilton takes a break.

41   Cyclists come in style.

42   Benchsitters Sterling Meacham and Amos Gaylord enjoy a treat.

43   The porch at "Cœur de l'Isle."

44   Brian Freeman, young rocker.

45   At the Children's Festival, Darryl Noke and Keith Dickerson.

46   Bessie and Clint Jenkins, of Whitman, visit Oak Bluffs on their 54th wedding anniversary.

47   Evangeline Berry's cat, Sena.

48   The last of the tent cottages in Vincent Park.

49   Shadows cast on the Walburton cottage, Rural Circle.

50   Summer interior.

51   The Bishop Haven cottage, where President Grant visited, from across Clinton Avenue.

52   Abby peers out the screen door of "Small Frey."

53   Ornamental trim details, the Ganz cottage on Hebron Avenue.

54   The Halls' cottage at twilight, Baylis Avenue.

55   Triple ruby windows aglow, Potter cottage, Trinity Park.

56   The Grand Illumination of the Tabernacle.

58   Vale Coffer-Shabica.

59   *Adrienne Almeida and friend paint a lantern.*

60   *Nancy Blank and Sam.*

61   *Julie Immelt.*

62   *Monica Carrie Tivey hangs lanterns for Illumination.*

64, 65 *Illumination lanterns.*

66   *Esmeralda Swindle's cottage on Trinity Park.*

67   *Bill Allen tends porch lanterns.*

68, 70 *Keith Lockhart directs the Boston Pops Esplanade Orchestra.*

71   *Sarah Schiffler, pianist, performs at the Community Sing.*

72   *The Parsons' Plunkers.*

73   *Tom Gervais and Noreen Baker dance to the Martha's Vineyard Swing Orchestra.*

75   *Interior view of the Tabernacle structure.*

77   *Courtney O'Connor, Jackie Maitland, and Tracy Monteith, along with the Doyle family, attend a Wednesday evening Community Sing.*

78   *Lengthening shadows of autumn, Trinity Park.*

81   *Many winners from the Fair.*

82   *John and Roberta Lowe.*

83   *Fall display of bittersweet at the Robinson Cottage on Clinton Avenue.*

84   *An afternoon bike ride past the Jecoy cottage on Butler Avenue.*

85   *In Wesleyan Grove, autumn leaves fall on the Robinson cottage.*

86   *Interior of* Wee Hoos.

87   *Baskets in a Trinity Park kitchen.*

88, 89 *Porch details.*

90   *Amy Potter's country kitchen.*

91   *Summer interior, Trinity Park.*

92   *Dot the cat was named for Dorothy West, Oak Bluffs author, and the last surviving member of the Harlem Renaissance.*

93   *Fall still life at "Captain's Corner."*

94   *The Shabica cottage features a unique roof-peak trim.*

95   *Shadows cast on the Hacker cottage, Cottage Park.*

96   *A perspective view through the porches lining Trinity Park.*

97   *Pink screen doors dress the Downey cottage, "Lavender and Old Lace," on Trinity Park.*

98   *Autumn's golden light, Trinity Park.*

99   *Etched door window at the McKenna cottage, Trinity Park.*

100   *The Tabernacle in snowfall.*

103   *George Martin on a cozy winter's day.*

104   *Ocean Park at sunset.*

105   *Winter sunset reflected along Lake Avenue.*

106   *The Gerrards' in deep winter.*

107   *The "Wooden Valentine" in winter.*

108   *"Bell Buoy" and "Captain's Corner" on a winter's day.*

109   *Mrs. Olsen's blue pots and pans.*

110   *A holiday wreath decorates the Alexander cottage on Trinity Park.*

111   *Snow-covered balcony of the Roe cottage, Wesleyan Grove.*

112   *The Whitney cottage glows with holiday lights in Cottage Park.*

113   *Those who remain have their own winter Illumination.*

114   *"Tall Timbers" on Allen Avenue.*

115   *The Fergusons' snow-covered porch in Wesleyan Grove.*

116   *The Collisons' shed sheltered in the snow.*

117   *Gothic-arched window of the Long cottage, Clinton Avenue.*

118   *The Tabernacle through snow-covered branches.*

SOURCES AND ACKNOWLEDGMENTS:

Hebron Vincent, early historian; Henry Beetle Hough, whose *History of Martha's Vineyard* is only one of many publications about island history; the *Dukes County Intelligencer*, published by the Dukes County Historical Society; Ellen Weiss, whose *City in the Woods* is a good source for Camp-meeting history; and the Martha's Vineyard Camp-meeting Association.
Special thanks to the cottage-dwellers and storytellers.

We would also like to thank: Ann Nelson her for encouragement and for pointing us in the right direction; Sharon Danley for her support in getting this project off the ground and for her dedication in the creation of our presentation dummy; The Martha's Vineyard Times for their technical support; our friends and families for all their encouragement. A very special thank you to Carl Zahn for his masterful layout and design, and to David Godine for his enthusiasm as publisher.

This is an Imago Mundi Book
published by David R. Godine Publisher, Boston, Massachusetts
designed by Carl Zahn
and printed by South China Printing Company Ltd., Hong Kong

This book is set in Monotype Bell, first cut in 1788 by Richard Austin, a professional engraver who produced it for John Bell of London, a publisher, bookseller, typefounder, and printer whose avowed ambition was "to retrieve and exalt the neglected art of printing in England." The digital version used here is based on the types recut by Monotype Corporation of London in 1930, under the supervision of Stanley Morison.